Acknowledgements

Thank you to my friend and pastoral leader, Penny Smith, for giving up your time to read through this devotional and offering editing suggestions.

Thank you to my husband, who has always supported me in my blogging and writing.

Thank you to family and good friends, you know who you are, for all the encouragement and support you have given me in my writing.

Thank you, Lord God for giving me a love for your reading and studying your Word and giving me the desire to share what I have learned from you with others.

Vicki Cottingham

Contents

INTRODUCTION

I initially wrote this Advent Devotional for my blog.

At the time I felt led to find out more about the advent wreath and what the candles represent. Being from a non-denominational background we don't have an advent wreath in the church I attend. As I found out more, an outline for my Advent devotionals began to take shape.

I discovered that traditionally there are four candles around the wreath and a candle is lit on each of the four Sundays before Christmas. Each candle represents something different.

The first candle is for hope and is called 'The Prophet's Candle' as many of the prophets, such as Isaiah, for example, wrote about and waited in hope for the coming Messiah. The theme for my first week of devotionals is **Hope – Prophesy and Promise.**

The second candle is for faith and is called 'The Bethlehem Candle'. The theme for my second week of devotionals is **Faith – Preparation and Waiting**.

The third candle is for joy and is called 'The Shepherd's Candle. The theme for my third week of devotionals is therefore **Joy**.

The fourth candle is for peace or love and is called 'The Angel's Candle'. I have chosen the theme of **Love and Worship** for this final week of devotions.

Each week consists of six daily devotionals which then leaves you with one day in the week to either catch up if you have missed a day or time to reflect on the week as a whole.

In each devotional I reference Scripture, provide a short thought and finish with something for you to think about. There is also space for you to journal at the end of each day should you wish to.

You can use this devotional in your own daily quiet time with God. I suggest you begin the day after the first Advent Sunday. Alternatively, as there are a total of twenty-four devotions you may like to begin on the 1st December. To take it further you may like to discuss it with a friend who is also reading it and meet once a week to share what God has been teaching you. You could also use it in a small group and meet weekly to go through the material and share what you have been learning.

WEEK 1: HOPE - PROPHESY AND PROMISE

DAY 1

Genesis 3:15 "And I will cause hostility between you and the woman, and between your offspring and her offspring. He will strike your head, and you will strike his heel." (NLT)

The first prophesy given by God concerning Jesus is found in the very first book of the Bible.

Adam and Eve had a perfect relationship with God, but then they gave in to temptation and sinned. You can read about this in Genesis 1-3.

After they had sinned, it would seem that there was no hope because their sin separated them from God. Their situation was one of hopelessness – their relationship with God was damaged, as was their relationship with one another and with nature. They could do nothing to redeem it, even though they tried. They had made a mess of their lives.

But here, in *Genesis 3:15* we have the promise of the Messiah, God's promise of hope for all people, for all time. This verse refers to God's plan to redeem his people, to send Jesus as their Saviour.

God's plan of a Saviour for all became reality that very first Christmas recorded for us in the Bible, many years after the events recorded in

Genesis. God sent Jesus to be the hope of the world. He entered our mess – mine and yours – in order to redeem us and bring us once more into a loving relationship with God.

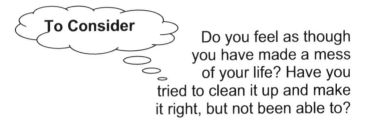

To Consider Do you feel as though you have made a mess of your life? Have you tried to clean it up and make it right, but not been able to?

Is there something you need to hand over to Jesus and ask him to redeem, such as a situation or a relationship?

"May the God of hope fill you with all joy and peace as you trust in him, so that you may overflow with hope by the power of the Holy Spirit. Romans 15:13" (NIV)

Journal

DAY 2

"Out of the stump of David's family will grow a shoot - yes, a new Branch bearing fruit from the old root." Isaiah 11:1 (NLT)

"'For the time is coming,' says the Lord, 'when I will raise up a righteous descendant from King David's line. He will be a King who rules with wisdom. He will do what is just and right throughout the land. And this will be his name: 'The Lord Is Our Righteousness.' In that day Judah will be saved, and Israel will live in safety.'" Jeremiah 23:5-6 (NLT)

In these Bible passages we have God's prophesy that his son, Jesus would be a descendant of David.

In *Matthew 1:1-16* we see this prophesy fulfilled. Jesus was born to Mary and Joseph and so was from the line of Judah, the line of kings. He was a descendant of King David.

Jesus came as a baby, but he is also the King of Kings, the Eternal King. We can look forward to the day when he will rule over everything as our Everlasting King.

This Christmas, as you think about Jesus coming into the world as a baby, also remind yourself of his kingly status.

 **To Consider** Is Jesus King of your heart? Or does another person or thing hold that place in your heart which is meant just for him?

Do you need to reinstate him now as King in your life and what would that look like in practice?

Journal

DAY 3

Read *Luke 1:67-79*

Zechariah, filled with the Holy Spirit, gives a prophesy in these verses. He prophesies on the day John the Baptist is born that he will be a prophet of God, the one who will prepare the way for the Lord Jesus Christ.

God had a purpose for John the Baptist and a part ready for him to play even before he was born or grown up. The Bible is full of accounts about men and women who were chosen by God for a specific purpose.

If God is the same today as he was then, and I believe he is, then he is still choosing people today for his plan and purposes. Does it fill you with hope that God has chosen you and he has something for you to do which only you can do? It does me.

God chose John the Baptist to prepare the way for Jesus. We also can go about our day, using the opportunities when they arise to introduce them to Jesus. To prepare the way so they too can have an encounter with the living Lord.

 **To Consider**

Advent provides us with various opportunities to introduce others to Jesus.

What can you and I do to make Jesus known, not just as the baby who entered our world at Christmas time, but as the one who is the Saviour of the World, Immanuel, the light and hope of the world?

Journal

DAY 4

"All right then, the Lord himself will give you the sign. Look! The virgin will conceive a child! She will give birth to a son and will call him Immanuel (which means 'God is with us').") Isaiah 7:14 (NLT)

Read *Matthew 1:18-25.*

God tells his prophet, Isaiah, to prophesy that Jesus will be called Immanuel, meaning God is with us.

In the passage in Matthew we read that Joseph, finding out Mary is pregnant makes the decision to divorce her. However, God sent an angel to him to reassure him that what was happening was fulfilling what God had spoken through the prophet Isaiah. This gave Joseph the confidence to be obedient to God.

The angel reminded Joseph of who this baby was: Jesus. The one who would save his people from their sins, and Immanuel, God with us.

In the busyness of Christmas, it can be easy to forget who we are celebrating is Immanuel, God with us.

 **To Consider**

What can you do this year to keep in the forefront of our minds that God is with us?

Spend some time meditating on the truth, "God with me".

Say the sentence out loud, emphasize a different word each time:
GOD with me.
God WITH me.
God with ME.

What thoughts come to mind as you say these words?

Try practicing the following Breath Prayer: *Immanuel … God with me.*

Journal

DAY 5

"But you, O Bethlehem Ephrathah, are only a small village among all the people of Judah. Yet a ruler of Israel, whose origins are in the distant past, will come from you on my behalf." Micah 5:2 (NLT)

Read *Luke 2:1-7.*

Mary and Joseph were from Nazareth in Galilee, but Micah's prophesy foretells that Jesus would be born in Bethlehem. We see the fulfilment of that prophesy in *Luke 2:1-7.*

God is Sovereign and his purposes and plans are always fulfilled. God uses a man who had no interest in God whatsoever, but is in political power at that time, to fulfil his plan for where Jesus would be born. God ensured Jesus was born at just the right time in history.

I find hope in these passages as I see how God works everything together for his purposes. It may not have been ideal from Mary and Joseph's point of view, but God had it planned from even before the beginning and we see his plan unfold as we read the Bible.

God is one who can be trusted. He always, always, always keeps his word. He is the promise maker and the promise keeper.

Therefore, I can trust him when it comes to working his purposes out in my own life. Even though it may not happen as to when or how I might like it to. God is in every single detail; in the details we haven't even thought about.

To Consider

How does today's devotion bring you hope?

Have you experienced God as the promise maker and the promise keeper in your own life?

Which promises has he already fulfilled in your life and which are you still holding onto with hope?

Journal

DAY 6

Read *Isaiah 9:2-7* and *John 1:1-14*.

As you read these two passages, one from the Old Testament and one from the New Testament, compare them and consider their similarities. You may like to journal what you find.

Today, I want us to particularly concentrate on the names given to Jesus from the passage in Isaiah. On Day 4 we meditated on Jesus' name, Immanuel. Today we consider four other names given to him once again in the book of Isaiah. These are Wonderful Counsellor, Mighty God, Everlasting Father and Prince of Peace.

1. Wonderful Counsellor

If we know Jesus personally then we have access to all his wisdom and knowledge. If we go to him, he will give us wonderful counsel and excellent guidance. As the Wonderful Counsellor, Jesus is able to reveal to us the mind of God. No one can counsel, teach or guide us like Jesus can.

2. Mighty God

Jesus is our Mighty God and we can experience him as such if we will just let him in to whatever we're going through.

Jesus is our protector and our defender. He is for us, and because he is for us nothing and no one can stand against us. He is our refuge and our stronghold. We don't need to try to be strong on our own, we can run to him. We can receive his strength.

3. Everlasting Father

The idea behind these words is that Jesus is the Father of Eternity. He is the source or author of eternal life. Jesus is the source of my life and your life. He gives us the gift of eternal life. He loves us with an everlasting love, a love which is constant and unchanging.

4. Prince of Peace

Jesus Christ is our peace and gives us inner peace. When Jesus Christ lives in us and we live in him, then his peace will guard our hearts and minds. Ultimately, the peace I have, despite struggles and difficulties, is the peace which comes from knowing I have given my life to Jesus and handed control of it over to him.

 **To Consider** How do you think these names describe who Jesus is?

How has Jesus revealed himself to you as your Wonderful Counsellor, Mighty God, Everlasting Father, and Prince of Peace?

Spend some time meditating on *Isaiah 9:6-7* and ask God to speak to you through these verses. Journal what you sense God is saying. Consider writing a prayer based on your meditation.

Journal

WEEK 2: FAITH – PREPARATION AND WAITING

DAY 1

Read *Luke 1:26-38.*

We read in these verses the incredible message Mary receives from the Angel Gabriel telling her that God has chosen her to bear his Son.

With amazing faith, she responds, *"I am the Lord's slave…May it be done to me according to your word." v38* (HCSB)

I am so challenged by her faith in that moment. There is not yet physical evidence of what she is being told, but she takes God at his word.

Jesus, the word of God (*John 1:1*) is planted and growing within her and sustains her in her waiting.

I love the imagery of this because it also applies to you and me. God has given us his word. If we allow God to plant the seed of his word in our hearts it will grow and so too will our faith in him. Having faith in God and his word will sustain us in our waiting just as it did for Mary.

To Consider

Is there a particular promise from God which you have stored in your heart?

Will you exercise faith in the waiting?

Meditate on *Luke 1:45 "Blessed is she who has believed that the Lord would fulfil his promises to her!"* (NIV)

"Faith is the assurance of things you have hoped for, the absolute conviction that there are realities you've never seen." Hebrews 11:1 (VOICE)

Journal

DAY 2

Read *Luke 1:39-45, 56.*

Mary visited her cousin, Elizabeth, who was also expecting a child given to her by God.

In the early stages of her waiting and preparing to be a mother, Mary needed to be with someone who knew where she was coming from. Someone who would understand and could relate because she was in a similar situation, just a bit further on in her journey.

What a support and encouragement they must have been to each other. They could share what was on their hearts without fear of judgement, criticism or misunderstanding. How it must have helped them both in their journey of faith.

Whilst you and I wait for God's word to be fulfilled in our lives, it's important to be surrounded with people who understand and care. We need people in our lives who will speak words of encouragement and will journey with us. We also need to be that person for others.

To Consider

Do you have an Elizabeth friend in your life? If you haven't, ask God to bring that friend into your life.

How can you be that kind of friend to someone else? Is God laying on your heart someone you can offer that kind of friendship to?

Meditate on the following verse:

"And let us be concerned about one another in order to promote love and good works, not staying away from worship meetings, as some habitually do, but encouraging each other, and all the more as you see the day drawing near." Hebrews 10:24-25 (HCSB)

Journal

DAY 3

Read *Luke 2:25-35*.

Simeon is a great example to us of faithful waiting. I don't know how old he was when God gave him the promise that he would not die before seeing the Messiah with his own eyes, and I don't know how many years he had to wait for the fulfilment of God's promise. But I do know he waited in faith.

It can be hard to wait faithfully when there's no end in sight. All we can do is keep holding on and keep believing that God is true to his word.

I'm sure on the days Simeon struggled to hold on to faith he would remind himself of God's word to him.

We can do the same when we've waited for years and there's still no answer. I like to write down anything I believe God has said to me so I can return to it when I'm tempted to give up. Reminding myself helps me to persevere in the waiting.

When Simeon saw the fulfilment of God's promise, his first reaction was to praise God.

Simeon's example is such an encouragement and challenge to me to wait with faith, to recognise God's hand in what he's accomplished in my life and to praise him.

 **To Consider**

What can you learn from Simeon's example? Is there an encouragement or a challenge for you to take away?

Meditate on the following verse:

"This vision is for a future time. It describes the end, and it will be fulfilled. If it seems slow in coming, wait patiently, for it will surely take place. It will not be delayed." Habakkuk 2:3 (NLT)

Journal

DAY 4

Read *Luke 2:36-48.*

Like Simeon, Anna too showed faithfulness in waiting. She was dedicated to serving God in the temple. I imagine many of her prayers and times of fasting were focused on asking God to redeem Israel, to bring to earth the Saviour of the world.

That day, Anna was privileged to see the start of the answer to her prayers.

"At that very moment…" v36 (HCSB). God orchestrated it for Anna to be at the right place, at the right time, so she could see God's answer with her own eyes.

Throughout the Bible we have many examples of God acting 'at just the right time'. Do you have faith to believe God will also act at just the right time in your life too? He will ensure we are right where we need to be to see his plan for us unfold.

Like Simeon, Anna responded to God with thanks and praise giving. She also shared the good news with those around her.

Just like Simeon and Anna waited faithfully for the promised Messiah, we now wait for his promised second coming. The challenge for me from Anna's example, is will I share with those around me about the good news of Jesus or will I keep it to myself?

Anna continued to serve God in her old age. Age is no excuse for us not to faithfully continue to serving and loving God.

Meditate on the following verse:

"I wait [patiently] for the LORD, my soul [expectantly] waits, and in his word do I hope."
Psalm 130:5 (AMP)

Journal

DAY 5

Read *Matthew 24:36-44.*

In the advent season we remember not only that it is a season in itself of waiting and preparation, but that we are also in a season of waiting and preparation for our Lord Jesus' second coming: when he will come, not as a baby this time, but as our Eternal King.

As no one knows the date when this will be (see *v36*), we need to live in preparation, so we are ready for that day.

The lead up to Christmas is always a busy time of preparation. I like to be as prepared as possible (and get others in the family to help too), so when Christmas Day arrives, I am ready to enjoy the day.

As we prepare, we are actively waiting for that special day. This is also important when we're waiting for Jesus to come again. As a Christian, do I think, "I'm a Christian, I know I'm going to heaven, so all I need to do is wait and pass the time" or do I consider how to best use the time I have whilst I wait? Do I share the love of God and the good news about Jesus? Do I seek to become more like him? Do I love others the way God loves them? Do I use my spiritual gifts to encourage and build others up?

The advent season can be a difficult and lonely time for many people. If this applies to you, you may find it helpful to spend some time thinking about God's promise that one day Jesus will come again.

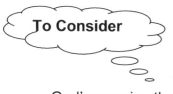

To Consider

During this advent season take some time to encourage yourself in God's promise that Jesus will come again.

Meditate on *John 14:2-3 "In My Father's house are many dwelling places; if not, I would have told you. I am going away to prepare a place for you. If I go away and prepare a place for you, I will come back and receive you to Myself, so that where I am you may be also."* (HCSB)

Journal

DAY 6

Read *Revelation 21:1-4.*

As a child, leading up to Christmas I can remember thinking, "I do want Jesus to come again, but not until after Christmas." I didn't realise until a few years ago, I had actually expressed that sentiment to my parents too! (I was blessed to have been brought up in a Christian home where God's Word was taught.)

As a child I was looking forward to opening my presents on Christmas morning and everything else that makes the day exciting. But it would be very sad if that was still my perspective today.

For me, knowing there is a place promised for me in heaven (as we considered yesterday) trumps any gift I could possibly be given at Christmas.

Today's passage is one of my favourites about heaven.

As Christians we have the presence of Jesus with us all the time, we experience his love, his peace, his comfort, his strength and so much more. However, this does not mean we are exempt from the trials, difficulties and pain in this life.

But I am able to endure and persevere when, alongside God's presence with me now, I know I will one day live in heaven, and there I will be free from difficulties, pain, death and sorrow. In the midst of my life here on earth I have something better to look forward to.

To Consider

Listen to the song, "I Can Only Imagine" by MercyMe. (You can listen to it on YouTube.)

Meditate on *Revelation 21:3-4*. What do you hear God saying to you from these verses?

Journal

WEEK 3: JOY

DAY 1

Read *Luke 1:5-25.*

Today I want us to focus on Elizabeth's part in the story.

For the Jews, a woman's purpose was to marry and be a mother. How hard must it have been for Elizabeth all those years not to have conceived a child, not to have fulfilled her purpose? What sorrow she must have known. She must have got to the place where she believed her dream of being a mother, her life's purpose, would never be fulfilled.

Yet God had heard the prayers of Elizabeth and Zechariah (v13) and he had watched as they lived a life of faith together. And God decided that now was the time for their prayers to be answered.

The Angel Gabriel said to Zechariah in v14, "*There will be joy and delight for you, and many will rejoice at his birth.*" (HCSB)

Elizabeth's story went from despair to hope, from sorrow to joy.

I believe God planted within Elizabeth the dream of being a mother. She thought the dream had died, but God is in the business of creating new

41

life where there seems to be no life. He has the power to resurrect that which is dead.

What joy Elizabeth must have experienced as she felt her child grow and move inside of her. What joy for her as she witnessed God's answered prayer as that new life grew within her.

Have you got a dream within you that you believe was planted there by God? But has yet to be fulfilled. Have you reached a point in your life where it seems that dream is dead and buried?

Will you take encouragement from Elizabeth's story? Despite everything, will you keep close to God as Elizabeth and Zechariah did? Will you choose to keep following God and loving him even if he doesn't give you what you long for?

Maybe now is the time when God will answer your prayer and breathe new life into your dream.

For Elizabeth, God's answer was even greater than she could have imagined or hoped for. Her son was John the Baptist – the one God chose to lead the way for God's own son. It may be that God's answer to your prayer will be even greater than you could have dreamed.

To Consider

Meditate on *Ephesians 3:20-21 "Now to Him who is able to [carry out His purpose and] do superabundantly more than all that we dare ask or think [infinitely beyond our greatest prayers, hopes, or dreams], according to His power that is at work within us, to Him be the glory in the church and in Christ Jesus throughout all generations forever and ever. Amen."* (AMP)

Journal

DAY 2

Read *Luke 1:39-56.*

Yesterday we considered Elizabeth's joy in finding God answered her long-awaited prayer for a child.

Today we read about her joy in welcoming Mary, her baby's joy (prompted by the Holy Spirit), and Mary's joy expressed in her song of praise in *v46-56*.

Mary was someone who, I believe, meditated on God's Word as we find in her praise song references to the psalms and Hannah's song of praise from *1 Samuel 2:1-10*. Mary had stored up God's truth in her heart and her song here reveals what is in her heart.

Her song of praise is called "The Magnificat", because as we read it, we see how her focus is on God and glorifying him. She recognises who God is and recognises also that she is his servant.

Perhaps for you, finding joy in this Christmas season is hard. Perhaps because of loneliness, loss of a loved one, a broken relationship, ill health etc.

Paul tells us to, "*Rejoice in the Lord always [delight, take pleasure in Him]; again I will say, rejoice!" Philippians 4:4* (AMP)

When we have God's Spirit living in us, even when life is challenging, he makes it possible to rejoice in God.

To Consider Take some time to pause and reflect on who God is, what he means to you and all he has done for you. Think about writing your own song or prayer of praise in your journal.

You may like to meditate on one of the following verses:

"You love Him, though you have not seen Him. And though not seeing Him now, you believe in Him and rejoice with inexpressible and glorious joy, because you are receiving the goal of your faith, the salvation of your souls." 1 Peter 1:8-9 (HCSB)

"Now may the God of hope fill you with all joy and peace as you believe in Him so that you may overflow with hope by the power of the Holy Spirit." Romans 15:13 (HCSB)

"So you also have sorrow now. But I will see you again. Your hearts will rejoice, and no one will rob you of your joy." John 16:22 (HCSB)

Journal

DAY 3

Read *Luke 1:57-58.*

When Elizabeth's friends, neighbours and relatives hear she has given birth to a son, they join with her, rejoicing.

It's a wonderful thing to have people around us who will celebrate with us; who will join us in our joys and our sorrows.

As a child, one of the things I really enjoyed was having our grandparents stay with us for the night of Christmas Eve. I loved that they would be there in the morning when I woke up, ready to celebrate Christmas Day together, and share in the giving and receiving of presents.

Being able to celebrate a special occasion with others who rejoice with you makes the occasion even more precious.

Who can you share some advent joy with this year? How will you celebrate? Often, we can put ourselves under pressure to go all out in celebrating but in the process we can become overwhelmed and feel like any joy we had has been sucked out of us.

Sometimes it can be the simple things which can bring us the most joy, for example, meeting up with a friend for coffee and a mince pie, going out one evening with the children to see the Christmas lights around the town, hosting a bring and share meal.

 **To Consider**

What simple thing could you do with or for another to bring you both joy?

Meditate on the following verse and what that might look like in practice: *"Rejoice with those who rejoice; weep with those who weep."* *Romans 12:15* (HCSB)

How can you be there for someone you know is struggling at this time of year?

Journal

DAY 4

Read *Luke 2:8-15.*

But the angel said to them, "Don't be afraid, for look, I proclaim to you good news of great joy that will be for all the people". v10 (HCSB)

"Glory to God in the highest heaven, and peace on earth to people He favours!" v14 (HCSB)

I love that the angels came to shepherds to proclaim the good news of Jesus' birth. The shepherds were ordinary people, they weren't people of status, they didn't hold important positions in society. They were people like you and me. They were important to God and were the first people to be told the good news of Jesus' birth which was to bring great joy for all people.

This great joy is something you and I can experience because Jesus came to earth to be your Saviour and mine. Having Jesus in our life means life will never, ever be the same, and that's a good thing.

We can know what real joy is even in the midst of the humdrum of ordinary life. Even in the midst of difficulties and trials we can experience the joy of the Lord. It's a joy which cannot be manufactured and it's a joy which is grown in us by the presence of God's Holy Spirit living within us. (See *Galatians 5:22-23*)

Not only can we experience his joy, we can also experience his peace, as it says in *v14* from today's reading. It's a peace which comes from having a restored relationship with God.

To Consider Meditate on *John 14:27 "Peace I leave with you; My [perfect] peace I give to you; not as the world gives do I give to you. Do not let your heart be troubled, nor let it be afraid. [Let My perfect peace calm you in every circumstance and give you courage and strength for every challenge.]"* (AMP)

What joy and peace have you known since having God in your life? How can you hold onto that joy and peace during the busy season of Christmas? If you find yourself overwhelmed or stressed this Christmas period what changes can you make to restore your sense of joy and peace?

Journal

DAY 5

Read *Luke 2:16-20.*

The joy the shepherds felt on seeing Jesus was just too great for them to keep to themselves. I can imagine them on their way back to take care of their sheep, talking excitedly about it amongst themselves and sharing it with everyone they met (see *v17-18*). Their joy erupted into praise and glorifying God, "*The shepherds returned, glorifying and praising God for all they had seen and heard, just as they had been told." v20* (HCSB)

Children can often be full of joy and wonder and can be almost bursting to share their joy with others. Yet, as we grow older, we can lose that sense of joy, awe and wonder, and we can tend to keep it to ourselves, rather than sharing it with others.

This good news of great joy is far too good for us to keep it to ourselves. Christmas provides us with a great opportunity to share our joy with those who don't yet know Jesus as their Saviour. Those who perhaps wouldn't usually come to church through the year may be more open to coming to Christmas celebration services, such as Carols by Candlelight or a Nativity Service which includes their children, or a Christmas Morning Service.

 **To Consider**

In what ways can you share the joy of Christmas this year with friends and family?

Journal

DAY 6

I love to sing carols at Christmas. In fact, as soon as we reach the first day of November, I play my Christmas Carols CD.

One of my favourite carols is "Joy to the World" written by Isaac Watts. Although it was not originally meant for Christmas but was based on *Psalm 98:4-9* and focused on Christ's second coming and his Kingdom reign.

The line which really catches my attention and challenges me is: "Let every heart prepare him room".

I can be so busy preparing for Christmas and focusing on what needs to be done and when it needs to be done. Because of that I can easily ignore or forget the state of my own heart. I forget I need to prepare room in my heart each and every day. I need to do it at the beginning of the day so there is room for him in my life throughout my day.

I think preparing my heart is about recognising what's in my heart which doesn't belong there and needs removing such as any sinful thoughts, attitudes and behaviour. It's about ridding myself of those things so there is room for Christ to reign in my heart as King.

Preparing my heart is about surrendering to his will and following his plan for my day. Putting him first and allowing nothing and no one to take his place.

When I prepare room in my heart for him then I experience the joy and peace which he longs for me to know.

 What can you do to prepare your heart for Jesus this year?

How will you ensure there is always room for him in your life?

Meditate on *Ephesians 3:16-19 (NLT)* *"I pray that from his glorious, unlimited resources he will empower you with inner strength through his Spirit.* [17] *Then Christ will make his home in your hearts as you trust in him. Your roots will grow down into God's love and keep you strong.* [18] *And may you have the power to understand, as all God's people should, how wide, how long, how high, and how deep his love is.* [19] *May you experience the love of Christ, though it is too great to understand fully. Then you will be made complete with all the fullness of life and power that comes from God."*

Journal

WEEK 4: LOVE AND WORSHIP

DAY 1

John 3:16-17 "For God so [greatly] loved and dearly prized the world, that He [even] gave His [One and] only begotten Son, so that whoever believes and trusts in Him [as Saviour] shall not perish, but have eternal life. [17] For God did not send the Son into the world to judge and condemn the world [that is, to initiate the final judgment of the world], but that the world might be saved through Him." (AMP)

I like receiving gifts. The gifts that mean the most to me are the ones which have had a lot of thought put into them. The giver knows me and loves me so they know just what I would like to receive.

God has given you and me the greatest gift of all. He gave us this gift because he loves you and me so much and he knew just what we needed and wanted, even though we didn't realise it at the time. God gave generously, whilst knowing some of us would reject his precious gift.

What is your response to his gift? Have you received it with gratitude and thanks? Do you treasure this precious gift, or do you take it for granted?

Perhaps something is holding you back from accepting it? Do you think you're not worthy to receive such a gift? None of us are. God gave his love gift not because of who we are or because of anything we have done. He gave it because of who he is. God is love and as such he loves to give us good gifts.

To Consider

This Christmas spend some time thinking about all the gifts you have received from God, beginning with the gift of his dear Son. (You may like to make a list of all God has blessed you with.) Think about the way you have received each of his gifts and how you have treated what he has given you.

What would you like to say to God regarding his gifts to you? (It may include both thanks and confession.)

Has anything changed within you as a result of this time of consideration and communication with God?

Journal

DAY 2

Read *1 John 4:7-19*.

As much as I love to receive gifts, I also enjoy giving them. When my children were younger and believed in Father Christmas, I loved to secretly buy them presents and then watch them excitedly open them on Christmas morning believing they were presents they had received from Father Christmas. Seeing their joy brought me joy too.

Yesterday we looked at how God has given us the greatest gift of all – his Son, Jesus Christ.

In today's reading we look at this some more and realise that because God has also given us the gift of his Holy Spirit, we are able to love others the way he loves us. We would never know how to love God or others if he had not shown us love first.

You and I have been given so much by God. We have been blessed abundantly by him. It's our love for him that spurs us on to share those blessings with others.

We can show God's love to others in so many ways. It doesn't necessarily mean wrapping a gift for them this Christmas (although this may be a part of it). It can be something such as:

- giving another person your time and attention;
- listening to them;
- chatting with someone you wouldn't normally chat with;
- welcoming them at church;
- doing their shopping for them;
- fixing a broken shelf;
- writing them a note or a card;
- baking them a batch of mince pies.

To Consider

To whom might God be asking you to show his love? Be open to the prompting of his Spirit. How might you go about showing this person love? Ask him to plant the idea in your mind and to help you be creative and imaginative.

Meditate on *1 John 4:16*. Try reading it in various translations.

Here's the verse from The Passion Translation:

"We have come into an intimate experience with God's love, and we trust in the love he has for us. God is love! Those who are living in love are living in God, and God lives through them."

Journal

DAY 3

Read *Luke 2:8-14.*

Last week we looked at this passage through the eyes of the shepherds. Today I want us to think about it with regards to the angels.

"At that moment, the first heavenly messenger was joined by thousands of other messengers— a vast heavenly choir. They praised God.

Heavenly Choir: To the highest heights of the universe, glory to God!

And on earth, peace among all people who bring pleasure to God!" v13-14 (THE VOICE)

Can you imagine what it must have been like to see these angels expressing in song their praise and worship of God? It must have been a sight to behold!

I love to go to church and join with others singing worship and praise to God. When we lift our voices together God is glorified.

One particular service I enjoy going to at Christmas is our church's Carols by Candlelight Service. There is something very special about singing carols together and celebrating the birth of our Lord and Saviour.

It's so easy to get caught up in all the busyness of the season and to get taken in by the world's perspective of what Christmas is about. Joining with other Christians who love God and want to worship him through carols helps me to remember what Christmas is all about and how only God is worthy of my worship.

 What does it mean to you to meet with others to sing your worship to God? If you're not able to get out as much as you would like, take some time to listen to some Christmas carols.

Do you have a favourite carol? Why is it a favourite of yours? You may even like to research it a little and learn about the author and the reason why they wrote the song.

Journal

DAY 4

Read *Matthew 2:1-12.*

These wise men were scholars who studied the stars and it was through their interest in the stars God reached out to reveal to them Jesus as the King.

In this passage, and many others throughout the Bible, we see how God makes the first move to reach out and connect with people.

The wise men didn't know exactly who or what they were searching for, but as they searched Jesus is revealed to them as the true King. They set out with focus, determination and purpose and they were not disappointed.

"And it is impossible to please God without faith. Anyone who wants to come to him must believe that God exists and that he rewards those who sincerely seek him." Hebrews 11:6 (NLT)

The first thing they do when they see Jesus is fall on their knees and worship him.

We read in the passage how wise men came to worship Jesus:

"Entering the house, they saw the child with Mary His mother, and falling to their knees, they worshiped Him." v11 (HCSB)

Their actions revealed they believed Jesus to be both King and God. They then offered him their gifts.

To Consider

Like these wise men, will you too bow down before Jesus, recognising him as your Lord and King? Will you give him your allegiance?

Will you surrender to him and his will for your life? What does that look like in practice?

What one gift can I give him today?

Journal

DAY 5

Romans 12:1 "Therefore I urge you, brothers and sisters, by the mercies of God, to present your bodies [dedicating all of yourselves, set apart] as a living sacrifice, holy and well-pleasing to God, which is your rational (logical, intelligent) act of worship." (AMP)

As this verse shows us our worship is so much more than coming together at church to sing our praises and worship to God. The Amplified translation of this verse helps us to understand it a little better.

We worship God when we offer to him the whole of ourselves – body, mind and soul – as a living sacrifice.

The challenge for me is to do this on a regular basis, not just daily, but moment by moment. I know how easy it is for my living sacrifice to jump off that altar in preference for doing things my own way and living for self.

Another translation I sometimes like to read is The Message Paraphrase. Spend a few moments now reading and digesting this verse, as it is written in The Message:

"So here's what I want you to do, God helping you: Take your everyday, ordinary life—your

sleeping, eating, going-to-work, and walking-around life—and place it before God as an offering. Embracing what God does for you is the best thing you can do for him."

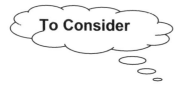

To Consider

Ask God to use this verse to speak into your life.

Think about the various parts of your life (as a spouse, parent, co-worker, friend etc) and how you can offer up to God each of these aspects of your life as a living sacrifice.

Is there an area in which you struggle more to do this? What might make it easier for you?

Journal

DAY 6

Revelation 22:20 "The One who testifies to these realities makes this promise:
The Anointed One: Yes. I am coming soon.
To which we say, 'Amen. Come, Lord Jesus.'"
(VOICE)

As a child, I loved the build up to Christmas. Writing a letter to Father Christmas, making cards and presents for family. Receiving cards from school friends and going to Christmas parties. Leaving a glass of milk and a mince pie for Father Christmas on Christmas Eve,

But then, at the end of Christmas Day, the inevitable anti-climax would hit me. All the excitement and build up for the day was gone, leaving me with this feeling of anti-climax.

There are times in life when the expectation and anticipation just do not match up with reality.

This will not be the case as we wait for Jesus to come again. The reality of seeing Jesus face to face, of loving him and worshipping him perfectly will far exceed our expectations, hopes and dreams. There will be no anti-climax.

 **To Consider**

Encourage your heart with the following Bible verse:

1 Corinthians 2:9 "No eye has seen, no ear has heard, and no mind has imagined what God has prepared for those who love him". (NLT)

As we come to the end of our Advent Devotional, let's focus on, and look forward to Jesus' second coming and respond together with:

"Amen. Come, Lord Jesus."

Journal

About the Author

Vicki lives in Eastbourne, in the South East of England and has been married to Jason for twenty-five years. They have two adult children.

Vicki attends Gateway Christian Church with her husband who is one of the Team Ministers. She is on the Preaching and Teaching Team.

God has given her a love for the Bible, for studying it and sharing it with others. She enjoys teaching about the Bible and helping others see how relevant it is to their lives in the 21st Century.

She enjoys relaxing by reading, crocheting and receiving lots of love from their dog, Rue.

If you would like to connect with her you can do so in the following ways:

- Twitter: @vickicotting14
- Facebook: @VickiCottinghamWriter
- Instagram: @VickiCottingham
- www.vickicottingham.com

Her Other Books

- Dear Friend… Volume 1
- Dear Friend… Volume 2

Both these devotional books have fifty-two weekly devotions to encourage, challenge and inspire.

- Praying Through Proverbs

All her books are available from Amazon or direct from her.

Printed in Great Britain
by Amazon